Some Thoughts
from the Other Side
of the

Rainbow

Charles William Esposito

ISBN 979-8-88943-243-2 (paperback)
ISBN 979-8-88943-244-9 (digital)

Christian Faith Publishing
832 Park Avenue
Meadville, PA 16335
www.christianfaithpublishing.com

Printed in the United States of America

I humbly and optimistically dedicate
this book to my Mom and Dad, God,
All Life forms, and Existential Peace

Preamble

The object of this book is an exercise in thought and an exploration of our consciousness. For only in knowing and growing ourselves can we truly make a difference in existence.

Mother Natures Maiden

It had to be one of the most enchanting days existence has known. There was a delicate beauty everywhere has known. From the clovers that were scattered about to the yellow-haired creature of unearthly loveliness who seemed to appear out of nowhere, clad in nothing more than a frail pixie garment—her presence couldn't be any more fitting.

She seemed to float as she walked, hardly bending the blades of grass that were caught in the path of her bare falling feet.

As she made her way through a green of botanical harmony, the sun rays came streaking through a thicket of trees and glistened off her golden mane, whose ends were busy being curled around her fingertips. As the streaks hit upon her gilded tresses, there was a glow set off that illuminated everything that surrounded her.

Smiling with every step taken, she marveled and became a part of all that was about her. Plucking the poppy from its stem, with a certain mildness in mind, she continued her walk. Inhaling the flower and enjoying its pleasant fragrance.

Coming up on a pool of water that lie at the edge of the green, she knelt beside it and started running her hand through the water, every now and then, she would pick her head up and look around, as if to make sure that nothing she was a part of had vanished. She seemed to really enjoy her solitude among the artwork of Mother Nature, as she sprinkled water randomly on various parts of her form.

Picking up a little stone and dropping it into the water, she noticed the circles of symmetry that were dispersed.

Observing this, she acknowledged by lifting her head skywards and peering into the stars began to speak.

"How come everything else that exists to my knowledge can't be as perfect as the rings in a pool of water? Maybe…someday. It's all too beautiful to be real. And yet it is. Or is it? If you think about it; doesn't anything real have to be created? And before something is created, doesn't it have to be thought of first? If so, isn't a thought essentially a dream? Incredible! That means that everything that's real was borne from a dream. Everything. Fantasy. Inconceivable. We're all living in a world of true fantasy, and there's probably only a handful of us that realize it, and even few of us that will admit it.

"To the handful…Good luck!"

"I knew I should've taken a walk today."

Embryo

From the moment that existence began and brought forth the universe, one other element was created at precisely that same instant. That element was and still is, until all things end and maybe even longer; *"Time."*

Time brings forth many things one of which is; *"Birth."*

Birth happens in many different ways at many different times. But no matter how or when it happens, the ultimate result is always the same. That what is known as *"Life."*

Life is a precious gift. It is something to be cherished. It brings forth a variety of many things in the time it is allowed to occupy in its existence. One thing it is certain to spawn is, *"Age."*

Age is essential; it is the length of time that life has to learn and grasp as much as it can.

One thing that is sure to be grasped is what is known as; *"Experience."*

Experience is the most treasured of life's gifts. It is the ingredient that refines, it brings forth; *"Wisdom."*

Wisdom is the key, it is the reason and the ultimate answer and peak of achievement. With the utmost quantity, there is no question that can't be answered. Not even that of existence.

Thus is the order of the; *"Embryo"…*

"Celestia"

Reminiscent of the rising sun, her soul shines in space; unbounded.

Controlling movements of serenity, her presence transfers tranquility.

Possessing the gift of demure, she controls her annoyances with power overflowing with sensitivity.

She radiates her affections; which are as soft as cotton, while showering you in excitability.

The present moment never to be forgotten. Her face will glow, like the full moon on a clear summer night.

And her hair will blow in the wind, bringing on total delight.

Wherever she goes and whatever she does; her appearance will do nothing.

Except bring a little piece of heaven into your life.

Warriors

See the children run the bases,
See the children lose their faces,
Watch the children one by one,
See them stumble as they run.

Watch the children throw the ball,
Having fun, one and all,
Watch the children storm the wall,
Watching their friends, as they fall.

See them run and jump through sand,
Never losing hold of the weapon in their
hand.

Hitting the ball and catching the flies
One runs bases, while another one dies…

A Way Out

In this world of atrocities and decadence, one must, in order to remain sane, create one's own little world within a world. One must be certain to keep this world about ones self no matter where one might be drawn. The temptations of decadence, contradiction, and atrocities are strong. One must forever be aware and fortified at all times in order to maintain a balance.

In this world, one must hold claim to nothing but positive energy, such as beliefs that are free from prejudices and bound to beliefs stemming from the roots of Love. One must have the insight to be able to read in between the lines; allowing one to separate truth from contradiction. Each time this task is accomplished, it is ones' obligation to reveal to others the treasured truth, which was severed from deceptive contradiction, along with the hope that these truths will be the means of bringing those lost in the dark out into the world of light.

To keep one's world vibrant with positive energy, one must seek out the forces of good. One must ally one's self with the likes of those who have gone out of their way for others and have asked for nothing in return. It is from these allies that true strength will come from. It is from these allies that loyalty will come from, helping to make one's world endure among the atrocities and contradictions that infest mankind. These allies will be known as the sentinels of consideration.

Along with the sentinels of consideration, one must also recruit the truth and beauty of the Artisans. It is from them that one's world will attain courage. It is through the energy being drawn from the feelings of the Artisan, that ones' world will forever carry on, for there is no known power that can quell feelings from speaking the truth. These allies shall be known as the Angels of Contention. These angels will forge ahead by using the images, music, and words of creativity they have been endowed with as tools to use against the forces of negative energy.

Along with the Sentinels of Consideration and the Angels of Contention, one must ally with those who forever question what surrounds them. It will be these that give meaning and strength along with a reason for the existence of the sentinels and angels. For every time one of them seeks an answer to a question, the sentinels and angels will be there. This adds new energy to the sentinels and angels by allowing them to expel positive energy, by helping those with the questions find the answers.

Through this expulsion, the angels and sentinels are replenished ten-fold. This metamorphosis of positive energy is everlasting, keeping forces of positive energy ever vibrant. For this reason, we shall call the allies of questions the bearers of perpetual strength.

When one builds this world with the honest hope for mankind as his perspective, one can do nothing but add more strength to the positive energy that exists within the universe; allowing the negative energy of atrocities, decadence, and contradiction that exists, to eventually dissipate to nothingness, bringing mankind back to a state of purity and righteousness.

Dove

Soar away, into the
Sun, my love.
Soar away, as free as
The Dove.
Take yourself away and
Do what you must.
But always know, there's
Someone you can trust.
'Cause, when it comes to
Dove, there is no other
I could ever possibly
Love…

"Bewildered"

Where are the lawmakers
And setters of examples?
Lost in a time gone by; or
Protected by the gamekeeper
Of antiquity?
Who's to sort the truth
From contradiction?
Children without guidance
Drown in obscurity.
No more prophets and no
More disciples.
Only children, utilizing
Their scruples.
Humanity struggles and
Survival looks dim.
Folly overtakes reality
While the children wrestle
To win…

Arcadian Sun

There it stood. In all its awesome magnificence. Bigger than any city known to man.

The shape was similar to an octopus. There was the round center and the tentacle-like structures, which extended out of its sides. In the center of the complex, reaching upward, was a structure that resembled a silo with multiple levels. The complete structure was totally transparent.

On the outside perimeter of the complex, arranged in a triangular pattern, stood three looming towers. The towers stretched as high as the silo structure. About a hundred feet past the towers and directly aligned with one of the soaring spires stood a crystalline-topped pyramid.

What this extraordinary monument did was draw the suns rays into its sparkling crown.

Instantly shooting the rays out and triggering the tower, which encircled the complex. The instant this happened, the most exquisite transformation ever occurred. The sun's rays took on the colors of the rainbow spectrum, traveling at the speed of light above the lucid complex. Once all the towers were triggered, they individually shot their colorful rays of light into the top of the silo and powered the complex. A world within a city harnessing the energy of the sun.

A whole metropolis running off the power of a rainbow…

On "The Truth"

When the time comes for us all
To face up to our final judgment
We must be ready to answer for
What we've done. Whether right
Or wrong, justified or not.
The answer we set forth will
Set the stage for our future existence.

So when you give your answers, weigh
Them heavily. Ponder your thoughts
And control them as you speak.
For if you're not careful, you may
Never have the opportunity to ever
Again experience existence…

Coming to Terms

Reality
Is the misguided
Offspring
Of
Fantasy…

Dreamers and Lovers

As clouds cover sun,
Man and Woman gaze,
In each others eyes.
Clouds cry and dreamers
Are no longer dry.
Rain wraps the earth,
Lovers wrap each other.
Thus, bringing Nature's
Symmetry; full circle…

Stand Against The Devil's Gun

One wonders to himself; which way
Should I turn?
Should I think of myself and when
It comes to anything or anyone else;
Let them burn?
Who knows?
Should one go for the Almighty Buck,
Or should one strive for life, liberty
And the pursuit of happiness?
Is there happiness without the buck?
When one takes that stand, does he
Wind up in an abyss with nothing to
Grasp; not even a hand?
One wonders!
Can one really exist?
Somewhere along the journey of seeking

There will come a twist.
So fast; like the snapping of a wrist.
But who knows?
It's hard to believe without the buck
Nothing glows.
One wonders…

On Nuclear Weapons as a Deterrent to Evolution

In this day and age, every living being on Earth lives with the threat of total annihilation hanging over their heads. The emissary of this annihilation being Nuclear Weapons. Mankind has evolved beyond slavery and holocaustic atrocities, bringing the evolution of mankind two plateaus higher.

Even allowing the existence, of the thought of the concept of Nuclear War, deters the evolution of man to a degree that is analogous to that of the Roman days of barbarism. There are enough nuclear weapons existing in the world today to destroy the planet twenty times over. Why? According to the cosmic calendar, we've come so far in so little time. And we have the potential to go much farther. Why regress? As long as the threat of Nuclear Weapons exists, the evolution of man is catapulted back to its beginnings; labeling everything accomplished fruitless.

Unleashed, nuclear weapons would devastate all that exists. And it would do it in the most barbaric way ever conceived. They would disintegrate, burn, melt, poison, and mutilate. The evolution of man would be totally reversed to the complete opposite extreme of what we are capable of achieving.

Although it all supposedly started with an explosion, it would only be poetic that it is all halted the same way…

A Lady

A Lady is one of the
Female species, who
Is both beautiful without
And just as beautiful, if
Not more so, from within…

Once Upon a Reflection

Within the confines of my life, private, I ponder the universe around and within me. I seek to understand and am totally misunderstood.

And yet, it is like this in universes both in and out.

It's a game, it's a circle, it's a cycle. Torn between thought, emotion, and sub-thought a raging battle persists.

Violence in and out.

There is beauty. But there is also atrocity.

An existence of constant malevolence. A more strange and diverse game never existed…

The Game

Have all the Politicians
Of the world become so
Hung-up and lost in
Their game, that they
Didn't notice the rest of
The common people of the world
Have advanced in their ways
Of thinking, toward a more
Peaceful-minded Humanity.
Along the way maturing and
Coming to realize that the
Game of Politics can be both
Foolhardy and disastrous…

Milady Jane

What can you do, and
What can you say when
You see Milady Jane.
Milady Jane, Milady Jane,
Seeing you could drive a
Person insane.
Small pretty eyes and long
Dark mane. That's just a
Small part of
Milady Jane

Time

Just as the Past gives birth
To the Future; So too,
Does the Future; Spawn
The Past...

Serenity

Dreams are to the
Mind; what Music
is; to the ears…

On War (as Competition)

War is competition at its zenith. There is nothing wrong with war. So long as the means is harmless and the outcome is that of a positive nature; adding to the footsteps of man's destiny. War motivates, expels energy, and creates.

There is nothing wrong with competition. Competition, set to motion in the proper frame of mind, becomes spiritually exhilarating and extremely productive.

War, thus far, in this century and centuries prior, has not been set forth in the right frame of mind. Some of the philosophies may have been right, but always the weapons wrong.

Instead of knives, guns, bombs, chemicals, and missiles being used in competition to mangle, mutilate, and destroy, maybe there should be contests of Medical and Technological personalities that could benefit the universe instead of helping to destroy it.

Think of it. All the Nations of the World could have a global war every year.

With all beings benefitting from it…

"Train of Thought"

With a brilliance never before seen
the sun breathes life into everything
it touches.
Calculating the length of each day
like the butterflies' wings, it represents
time, that flies by with an unheard
flutter,
Leaping all bounds and as endless
as space itself.
The future breaks the barrier of the
past.
Leaving old thoughts behind, seldom
remembered.
Making way for new future thoughts
to grow…

The Maturity of America

The problem with America, that I find bothers me the most, is its maturity. Its past; its two hundred years of birth somewhere along the road of maturity has taken a wrong turn.

America was spawned from the roots of religious belief. These roots being Puritanism. Granted, these roots may have been too stringent, but there lies the road to maturity.

As the decades passed, these roots became more malleable, giving way to new waves of thought. Men of vision appeared before us like Franklin, Jefferson, and Paine. These men put their visions to use for the benefit of the inhabitants of the new world they were living in. They realized that the laws they were being governed under didn't benefit anyone except those doing the governing. So they went about putting their visions into action.

The first of which was to govern themselves and not be governed by some absentee monarch who had no idea about the way of life they had undertaken.

Once they had accomplished this, they went about making laws they would live by. In these laws existed religious overtones. Overtones, which if not overused, could only be of benefit to humanity. The keyword being *humanity*. Back then, even two hundred years ago, the first politicians of this country had the welfare of humanity in mind, which could have been put to better use if half the technology that exists today, existed back then. But, that must be part of the Master Plan. It's ironic that today we have the technology but not the controlled level of, if I may, uncorrupted thinking we had back then. I'm not saying there isn't anything being done for the sake of the people of this country or all beings on the planet. It's fortunate for those living in America that they happen to be living in the most moralistic country on the face of the Earth. The problem is that in the process of whatever is being done is happening among a nest of dishonesty and deception.

Years ago, we had presidents who left office bankrupt and in debt because they invested all the money they had, and all they could borrow, into the welfare of the United States. Today, we have presidents who are left with no other option but to resign from office, along with other politicians who are more concerned with filling their pockets instead of the minds and mouths of those who need it. If you add the power that the mass media has today, these kinds of politicians do not add much toward the Philosophy of Patriotism, which, due to past government actions, is almost nonexistent.

The game of Politics is not an easy one, but if it were played with a little more honesty and less deception, it could be a little easier. How could any politician expect the concept of an all-volunteer army to work when the people who are expected to volunteer are confronted with situations such as Viet Nam and Agent Orange? My personal belief is that the average person today doesn't want to or can't relate to the concept of war. What individual, in this day and age, wants to run around thousands of miles from home blowing the faces off of men, women, and children?

I think, at least in the minds of the citizen, that war is a dying institution and an archaic concept. Whether it is on a one-to-one or push-button basis.

There are too many lives that depend on the decisions that the leaders of this country make, and if they can't make these decisions without the existence of the concept of war, things remain disastrous. Realizing that there are other powers being dealt with, the United States and the world will eventually find the road to peace if we return to a common-sense way of thought instead of a power-hungry way of thought.

If the United States and the other nations of the world united their resources and knowl-edge without worrying about the power syndrome, every being would be able to live comfortably and believe in whatever philosophy they wanted to as long as it didn't do anyone any harm.

Maybe America should slowly revert back to isolationism and at the same time build from within until we get to a point of total self-preservation and then go back to being the protectors of the world.

If it's a thought that can be conceived, it is a thought that can be accomplished, especially with the technology and power of thought that exist within this country.

If this can be accomplished, not only this country but the world would benefit.

Again, this brings not only this country but the world of humanity to a level of maturity more symmetrical with the capabilities of its destiny.

Ones Self

Religiously, I am a
Peacemaker
Patriotically, I am a
Son of liberty
Sociologically, I am a
Maverick
Literally, I am a
Romantic
Musically, I am a
Classicist
Artistically I am a
Creatist
But above all else
Humanly, I am
Man…

Reality

We all lose from
The minute we're born.
And
We all have to go.
It's just a matter of
How and when.

Dreams Reality

Rockin' and reeling and doing their dealin'
Makin' their moves in a short span of time
Enjoying the rhythm and rhyme
It's only temporary as long as time deems
But if there's fun and joy with
laughter and screams
Then let the children enjoy the
reality of their dreams.

"The Gig"

It's a partying nite and the
bands gonna be hot
The boys set the stage hopin'
the woman are hot-to-trot
They take the instruments
and set them in place
Each one a vibed-up look on their face
They set the lights and arrange the amps.
Finishing their work and feeling like champs
The ladies arrive hoping to
fulfill their dreams
While boogying and dancing
among the musical screams
They all take their place around
the band and amps
Some of them ladies and some them vamps
Although one thing holds true for
the length of their dreams
They all want to have fun or so it seems.

"Sorrowful Sunrise"

As the sun peaks out and
the sand glistens gold
Children grow into adults and fall in love
Eventually growing old never knowing
what tomorrow will hold
Watching the clouds take form in the sky
Confused souls stare into each other's eye
Soaking away in their thoughts
they wonder why
Thinking of the past they smile
Thinking of the future they cry
Looking down at the sand they
reach for each other's hands
Briefly knowing joy under the
blue sky, tears begin to

Form in each other's eye and
thinking back on all the fun
Realizing now the three should be
one man, woman, and son.

Tubby

There once was a man who loved to eat
He grew so round he couldn't see his feet
He tried everything to slim down
But nothing worked and he felt like a clown
He tried to control whatever he ate
But still couldn't fit through a gate
Losing faith and hope, he tried jumping rope
But couldn't get his feet off the ground
Wondering if he was always
going to be round
He tried fruits and vegetables but
could never leave the tables
Not being able to resist
dessert, it got to a point
Where he couldn't wear a shirt
So the moral of the story is if you don't want

To become round, watch
what you eat and you'll
Be able to see your feet as
they leave the ground.

Searching

Trying to find the time
To make the time to make things rhyme
Questioning yesterday and
contemplating today
Alone at last, seeing how time has passed
And watching it flow
What's around the corner I really don't know.

Natures Wonder

The song from the stream brings about
Serenity and natures dream
When the sun shines bright the
flowers create a lovely sight
Their scent is so nice it's a joy to breathe
The winter arrives bringing with it the snow
Becoming ever colder, it brings on the ice
Ever so stunning, it sets nature aglow.

About the Author

Charles William Esposito was born on July 18, 1950, at Victory Memorial Hospital in Brooklyn, New York, to William and Rosalie Esposito. He spent the first twenty-seven years of his life living with epilepsy. He went to Parkway Elementary School and spent his high school years and graduated from Eastern Military Academy where he excelled in sports and leadership. He went on to earn an associate's degree from Nassau Community College. Then he went on to earn a bachelor's degree, graduating with honors. After graduation, Charles went on to retire from the United States Postal Service after twenty-two years and resides in Oakdale, New York.